Information Security for the Busy Entrepreneur or Manager

W. Frank Ableson

Copyright © 2017 navitend Press
All rights reserved.
ISBN-13: 978-1532957826
ISBN-10: 1532957823

Dedication

To anyone tasked with securing the enterprise, regardless of its size or scope.

Contents

Acknowledgments

Introduction

MISSION AND RISK

1. Mission

Hands-On

2. Assets, Vulnerabilities, Threats & Risk

Hands-On

3. Beyond Fire, Flood & Theft

Hands-On

4. User Threats

Hands-On

5. Risk: What Can We Do?

Hands-On

6. Risk Playbook

Hands-On

7. Controls

Hands-On

8. Control Implementation Categories

Hands-On

INFORMATION SECURITY

9. What is Information Security?

Hands-On

10. Confidentiality

Hands-On

11. Integrity

Hands-On

12. Availability

Hands-On

13. Denial of Service

Hands-On

14. Quantifying Risk via Business Impact Analysis

Hands-On

15. Owning & Classifying

Hands-On

16. Trade Secrets & Intellectual Property: The Secret Sauce

Hands-On

THE HUMAN ELEMENT

17. Common Cyber Threats

Hands-On

18. The People!

Hands-On

19. Staff Risks

Hands-On

20. Remote Access

Hands-On

21. Remote and Mobile Worker Risks

Hands-On

22. Data Loss Prevention

Hands-On

INDUSTRY

23. PCI-DSS

Hands-On

24. PCI-DSS Basics

Hands-On

25. HIPAA/HITECH

Hands-On

26. HIPAA/HITECH: The Big Rocks

Hands-On

INFRASTRUCTURE & ORGANIZATION

27. Physical Conditions

Hands-On

28. Wireless Network Security

Hands-On

29. Electronic Asset Lifecycle

Hands-On

30. Leased Equipment

Hands-On

31. Computer Disposal

Hands-On

32. Role-Based Security Management

Hands-On

33. Internet of Things & Industrial Control

Hands-On

34. Multi-Factor Authentication

Hands-On

35. Configuration and Change Management

Hands-On

SOFTWARE CONCERNS

36. Custom Software Development

Hands-On

37. Common Security Issues in Software

Hands-On

38. Software Operational Issues

Hands-On

39. Capability Maturity Model for Software

Hands-On

WRAPPING UP

40. Recommended Practices

Hands-On

41. Get Some Help and Try Not to Be So Gullible!

Hands-On

42. Be Open Anyway

Hands-On

About the Author

Acknowledgments

Thank you to the team at navitend for your diligence in serving our clients and leading them to Greener Grass.

Introduction

This book is intended to be read quickly as a means to come up to speed on the basic principles of Information Security.

There is no chapter that is an exhaustive or authoritative resource; rather, the content in each is meant to give the reader a brief introduction to a topic as well as a set of questions to ask him or herself to help improve the security posture of his or her organization.

Some chapters may not be relevant for all readers. For example, there are a few chapters covering details around software development. Your organization may not write custom software; however, you are encouraged to read the material anyway as it is a quick read and may have applicability to other areas of your business process which are not directly covered here. Similarly, your organization may not be a Covered Entity as defined by HIPAA/HITECH; however, there is value in understanding the principles and requirements of the healthcare industry. Implementing its best practices can bear fruit in the security planning of any organization—and as a consumer, you are impacted by HIPAA each time you interact with a healthcare professional or organization.

It is my desire that you find value in this work. Please feel free to pass it along. Security is a shared responsibility.

If you have questions or suggestions, please feel free to forward them to fableson@navitend.com. All constructive feedback is welcome.

MISSION AND RISK

1. Mission

What is your organization's mission?

No decision should be made without considering the mission of your organization. Your mission should act as a filter for every decision. There is no one-size-fits-all solution to the security challenges we face today. For example, the right solution for a multinational consumer goods company is likely not the one that fits a small private business or non-profit organization, though there will be some best practices performed by organizations of all sizes.

Hands-On

What is your mission in everyday language?

Is your mission written down for everyone on your team to see?

Is your mission baked into your culture or just a sign on the wall?

When was the last time your mission impacted a significant decision in your organization?

With the idea of your mission statement in mind, are there any decisions you have made for which you would like a "do-over"?

2. Assets, Vulnerabilities, Threats & Risk

We own and use assets—buildings, vehicles, computers, printers, mobile phones, tablets, software, websites, etc.

Assets also include key human relationships—employees, suppliers, vendors, etc. All assets have varying levels of vulnerabilities. Our organizations are threatened when there is a possibility of a vulnerability being exploited (intentionally or accidentally) to the harm of the asset itself, the task it performs, or the information it manages. Risk is the likelihood that a threat is realized and the subsequent impact upon the organization's ability to carry out its mission, and perhaps even the organization's very existence.

Hands-On

List the mission-critical assets in your organization.

For each asset, list any known vulnerabilities.

For each asset, think about what would happen if that asset were either unavailable for use or gone forever. If it were unavailable for use for an extended period of time, what would you do?

If your top assets were unavailable for three weeks, would you still be able to operate your business?

What would be the impact to your mission?

3. Beyond Fire, Flood & Theft

Traditional examples of threats include fire, flood, and theft.

In our generation, we now need to expand this list to include acts of workplace violence, terrorism, and cyber crime.

In the global digital economy, we can be robbed and never even know!

Not only are our physical and electronic assets at risk, but our reputation and goodwill in the marketplace carry significant value and therefore present non-trivial vulnerabilities.

Unfortunately, we learn about many vulnerabilities only after the damage has occurred.

At the extreme end of the risk continuum, our organizations may not survive, and the task of fulfilling our missions may be left to others.

Hands-On

What threats do you perceive related to your organization's reputation?

Can you think of any circumstances that would become an existential threat to your organization? Does that extend to your mission, or are there others carrying the burden alongside your organization?

Have you taken any steps to address these threats?

Are there others in your organization who possess the same clarity around this issue?

4. User Threats

As managers, we face the non-trivial threat of lost staff productivity with our teams distracted by their cell phones and social media.

Not only do we face the challenge of focusing on teams to work efficiently—social media and text/media messaging can be a source of data leakage.

The economy is shifting, as is the workforce. A mobile phone is more personal than an employee's handbag, so we have to tread carefully around these topics.

Some workplaces have taken the step of banning personal devices altogether; however, this is not an easy concept to introduce, particularly to a younger workforce.

Hands-On

How many employees (and sub-contractors, vendors, etc.) are in your organization on a day-to-day basis with a personal mobile device?

Does your organization have a written policy around the use of personal cell phones? Does your policy include clearly-defined sanctions for violation of your policy?

Do your business practices (i.e. employee onboarding, employee training, and vendor agreements) make your policies clear to all concerned parties?

Do you have critical information that should never be accessed by a personal mobile device—for example, the Personal Health Information of a client or patient?

Do you have a good sense of what is "healthy" use versus unhealthy use of mobile technology?

Do you have a practice of monitoring the mobile-generated and mobile-consumed content on your network?

5. Risk: What Can We Do?

There are three productive ways to deal with risk:

1. **Mitigate:** Reduce the risk. Every now and again we can actually "eliminate" a risk, but most often we simply reduce our risk exposure through directed actions.

2. **Transfer:** This is where we put in place a mechanism that compensates us if the risk is realized. This often looks like insurance. At times we can also effectively transfer risk by hiring appropriately-licensed individuals or organizations to deal with a specific risk.

3. **Accept:** Healthy people and organizations accept risk every day.

Hands-On

Have you recently quantified the risks present in your organization? Unless you can name them, you will have difficulty reducing them.

Who is responsible in your organization for risk-management?

What keeps you up at night?

Is there anyone else in your organization carrying this kind of burden? Is that by design?

Do you have a good working relationship with an insurance professional?

Do you have clarity on all professional and legal jurisdictions for which you are accountable?

6. Risk Playbook

1. Identify the threats and quantify the risks to the organization and its mission.

2. Reduce the risks with a budget (time & money) that is in line with the organization's mission.

3. Transfer the risk with a responsible amount of insurance. An insurance payout may help the business owner recover from a loss, but what about the mission? Can the organization really "reboot" with just a check? Maybe.

4. Accept the new, hopefully reduced, level of risk.

5. Rinse and repeat. This is a continuous process, not a one-time activity to mark as "complete" on a to-do list.

Hands-On

Run through the Risk Playbook for your organization.

Who on your team should participate in this process?

If you have team members responsible for risk management, have you given them adequate authority to affect change?

Schedule this activity on your calendar before reading on.

7. Controls

Controls counteract threats and reduce risks:

Directives encourage acceptable behavior; e.g., a sign.

Deterrents discourage bad behavior; e.g., a monetary fine.

Preventative controls prevent unwanted access; e.g., a lock.

Compensating controls react to loss; e.g., a backup plan.

Detective controls provide warning signals; e.g., a sensor or alarm bell.

Corrective controls provide a remedy; e.g., fix the problem.

Recovery controls restore the conditions; e.g., restore the data.

Hands-On

List the controls you have in place in your organization today.

Are they effective?

What additional controls do you think are missing?

Is your team properly trained with respect to the purpose and application of each of these controls?

Have you asked your team for input on additional controls?

8. Control Implementation Categories

Controls fall into three primary categories:

1. **Administrative:** This looks like management-established policies and procedures.

2. **Physical:** Locks, man-traps, fire-suppression systems, backup generators, etc.

3. **Logical or Technical:** Hardware and software implemented.

Hands-On

Review the controls you identified in the prior chapter. Categorize each of them as either administrative, physical, or technical.

Are all of your administrative controls adequately documented and communicated to your staff? Are they in line with employment laws?

Are your physical controls adequately maintained?

Are your technical controls up to date? Are they patched? Are they still relevant?

Do you have a process to review and update your controls on a periodic basis?

Do any of your controls unnecessarily impact the through-put of your organization?

Can you remove any rules which are unnecessary or burdensome? Remember, rules which are inconvenient are often ignored unless the community recognizes their purpose and value.

INFORMATION SECURITY

9. What is Information Security?

While there are lots of ways to describe Information Security, it can be summarized with a discussion around three terms:

1. **Confidentiality**

2. **Integrity**

3. **Availability**

We will address each of these in the subsequent chapters.

Hands-On

What does confidentiality mean to you?

Is there an industry-specific implication of "confidentiality" that makes it more relevant to your organization? For example, in the healthcare, banking, and intellectual property domains, confidentiality has (seemingly) more weight than in other business domains.

What happens to your organization when confidentiality is compromised?

What does integrity with respect to information mean to you and your organization?

What happens when there is a lack of integrity in your organization's information?

What does availability mean to you? What happens to your organization and its mission if the use of your data is unavailable for a short or long period of time?

10. Confidentiality

The primary concern with confidentiality is the unauthorized access and dissemination of your data.

Identity theft is a classic example, as is the loss of privacy of proprietary product plans. A list of your clients and their buying patterns is extremely valuable to a competitor. This data needs to be protected.

Commercial and nation-state espionage are no less important and are increasingly prevalent.

Industry and governmental compliance requirements place additional demands around confidentiality:

- **PCI-DSS** (Payment Card Industry Data Security Standard)

- **HIPAA** (Health Insurance Portability and Accountability Act)

What about your office copiers? Every photocopy on a modern copier or fax machine is stored to a hard drive. Old copiers don't go straight to the junk yard; they often wind up overseas. Are your driver's license and social security card floating through the digital underworld?

In the long-run, the SaaS model can be more costly from a strictly financial-analysis perspective. However, the attractiveness of "pay as you go" and the ability to fit into an "operational budget" as opposed to a "capital budget" plus an annual maintenance budget make SaaS the better option for many businesses. Additionally, the monthly fee approach provides many businesses the flexibility they need if they don't have the resources to manage a traditional software investment and use it to its full potential. Because many SaaS offerings are month-to-month with no long-term obligation, there is additional peace of mind to transition to another option without severe financial penalties.

Hands-On

Is your organization subject to an industry mandate such as PCI-DSS or HIPAA? Hint: if you have employees and deal in any manner with health insurance, you should act as if you are under the HIPAA/HITECH regulations.

What information, if in the hands of your competitors, would be catastrophic for your business?

Do you have a good understanding of which employees (and contractors) have access to your critical information?

Do you have a standard practice of encrypting all of your organization's laptops and tablet devices?

If your laptop were left on the train, what dire circumstance would await your company?

Do you travel internationally? Have you left your laptop in your hotel room when you went sight-seeing?

11. Integrity

We need to be able to trust our data. If a data record is modified in an unauthorized and untraceable manner, there is no end of the drama and damage that may ensue.

Here are some not-so-obvious examples of integrity being compromised:

- When you back up your data, how do you know that you have a good copy? Do you verify it? Do you periodically test that the backup is properly written, stored, and secured?

- When you download and install software, do you verify that it came from the correct source?

- When you enter your private information into a website, do you know that you are really at the correct site?

- When you design a product and use a low-cost integrated circuit from a little-known supplier, do you know that there is no "back-door" feature?

Hands-On

What data do you trust in your business without a second thought?

What would happen if that data were corrupted, either accidentally or by someone with malicious intent?

Could you wind up deploying assets to the wrong battlefield, or capital to the wrong market?

What data-integrity safeguards do you have in place today?

What additional safeguards can you quickly and affordably introduce?

12. Availability

The classic view of availability from an Information Security perspective is "data backup."

Backing up your data is necessary but not sufficient.

- If you cannot access your data, you cannot use it.

- If you cannot use your data, your ability to meet your organization's mission is severely impacted.

The longer you are unable to use your organization's data, the greater the impact on your organization's welfare and its mission.

Threats to the availability of our data have grown beyond the usual equipment failure, physical theft, accidental loss, fire, flood, and meteor strike. Now we also face cyber criminals looking to hold our data hostage.

Hands-On

Who is responsible for ensuring the availability of your organization's data?

Look beyond your primary day-to-day files: where else does your data reside? Think through each job function and team member. Where does their data reside? Think also of seldom-used data such as quarterly or annually reported information such as tax filings.

Do you have a means of backing up any of your crucial data that lives "in the cloud"?

When you do have offline backups of your data, are you securing them adequately?

Have you tested your backups?

If you accidentally went surfing with your cell phone in your pocket and all of the data were lost, is that data backed up in another location?

If all else fails, do you have someone to call in to help in a time of crisis?

13. Denial of Service

If your information assets are unavailable, your mission is compromised.

An increasingly common threat to the availability of your computing resources is a "denial-of-service" attack. A denial-of-service attack occurs when an attacker floods a network, server, phone system, etc. to the point where legitimate traffic cannot access the resource.

This is most commonly seen as a "distributed denial-of-service" attack, or DDOS. A DDOS looks like hundreds or thousands of computers simultaneously accessing a network. At best your website (or other resource) is slow or perhaps simply unavailable. Even worse, your data may be exposed to inappropriate viewers or even corrupted if hardware fails in an unexpected manner.

Depending on how your organization operates, a DDOS attack can range from being inconvenient to being an existential threat. For example, imagine the monetary impact to a company such as Amazon.com if customers cannot place orders for multiple hours or days at a time.

Hands-On

Is there a time-sensitive nature to the way your business operates?

Does the term "opportunity cost" come up in a risk assessment of your operation?

If your website or internal network were to be offline for an hour, would it cost your company revenue? How about the loss of purchasing opportunities?

For many organizations, this topic is equally relevant for voice traffic as it is for data traffic. Is your phone system capable of operating during a DDOS attack? Is your network traffic prioritized and segmented for voice service?

What steps can you take to improve your organization's resilience to a denial-of-service attack?

14. Quantifying Risk via Business Impact Analysis

You can be confident that there will be "bad days" when it comes to the circumstances around your business.

With that in mind, we're dealing with not "if," but "when" something bad happens related to your data and its use in your organization.

Spending some time to think and plan before an incident is crucial to the survival of your business.

The formal name for this step is a "Business Impact Analysis." You are studying the negative impact to your business as a consequence of an outage, loss, or other event.

Answering these questions helps to quantify your organization's risks and can provide guidance on what kind of budget is necessary for your risk mitigation and risk transfer steps.

Review your Business Impact Analysis no less than annually, and review it more frequently if there is a major change in your mission, your process, or key resources like your software platform or business partners.

When considering a new product or service offering, revisit your Business Impact Analysis before taking action, if at all possible. Map out your anticipated future reality and count the cost of mitigating any newly-introduced risk.

Hands-On

1. Inventory the functions, processes, and personnel/roles in your business. Rank them in order of criticality and do not neglect to explore key dependencies and interactions between them.

2. For each item identified, determine two things:
    a. Is there a "backup" process that can be put in place if the primary capability is "offline"? For example, can you bring a clipboard instead of a tablet to a service call? Can employees work from home? Is your staff adequately cross-trained, or do you have too much knowledge or skills wrapped up in one individual? Remember, that individual may be you!

    b. Determine the "Maximum Tolerable Downtime," or MTD, for each. Be realistic here; how long can you operate either with or without your "clipboard"?

15. Owning & Classifying

It is the responsibility of management to protect the organization's assets and its ability to operate.

- "Due care" means that your organization is employing the best practices for information security. These are the steps that a reasonable person can be expected to follow, provided that he or she has appropriate training. If you are unsure of what those best practices should be, seek guidance from someone who has implemented them in his or her own business, and/or hire a professional to assist.

- "Due diligence" is the management discipline of ensuring that your organization is exercising due care and working with business partners who do the same. Note that there is a difference between being in compliance because of your practices versus being "lucky."

- Data classification is the step of identifying all of the data which is managed in your business, what its sensitivity level is, who sees it, who manipulates it, etc. **Virtually all information security decisions rely upon the data owner (that's you!) making prudent decisions around data classification.**

Hands-On

As the owner/CEO of your business, the buck stops with you: you are the data owner. However, you may not be the "custodian" of the data on a day-to-day basis.

Referring to your previous inventory lists, name the data custodian(s) of each piece of information your business relies upon. Do you have a secondary resource to stand in for your primary custodian in the event that person is unavailable to manage the data for the organization?

Is the data in your organization clearly identified with respect to its sensitivity (classified, secret, etc.)?

16. Trade Secrets & Intellectual Property: The Secret Sauce

The most precious commodity for many organizations is their intellectual property. This comes in many forms; for example, design or process inventions for a marketable product or service (possibly secured by patents), trademarks, service marks, and copyrighted material.

More generally, a well-run organization has a documented set of processes and tools that govern their operations. Some of these processes and tools may be protected as "intellectual property" and some may not.

Non-disclosure agreement (NDA) documents are not a cure-all for preventing the undesirable effects of sharing information; however, it is a good practice to put an NDA in place when discussing your "secret sauce."

Two notes of caution:

1. If there is too much friction in transacting due to your NDA language, you may be left with no business partners. Weigh the relative risks.

2. If a potential business partner is offering an agreement that is very one-sided in his or her favor, it may be prudent to walk away rather than enter into an agreement that is a lifetime burden.

Hands-On

Inventory all intellectual property owned, controlled, or used by your organization.

Identify intellectual property used by your organization that is a key differentiator for the operation of your business.

Do you have a workable non-disclosure agreement to be executed by a prospective business partner?

Do you have a professional resource to assist you in matters relating to intellectual property?

THE HUMAN ELEMENT

17. Common Cyber Threats

Most attacks target *people*.

These attacks are most often email-borne. Phishing attacks are broadcast to many unsuspecting users, while Spear Phishing is an attack aimed at a specific, named target.

Beware of attachments. Ransomware is often delivered via a form of malware disguised as a picture or PDF attachment. If this takes hold and you do not have an adequate backup solution, you will need to break out your bitcoin to get your data back.

Other items to be mindful of:
Spoofed phone calls can trick you into divulging personal information.
Beware of clicking on links in your text messaging app as your mobile device may be remotely accessed and controlled.

Video surveillance may be watching you tap in your password or pin.

Increasingly, products are activated via voice commands. This means that our devices are *always listening*. Stop to think about that for a moment!

Hands-On

The best safeguard here is training for your staff. Is your staff trained and regularly reminded about these common cyber security threats?

Do you have an adequate data backup solution to mitigate catastrophic data loss due to user-targeted cyber crime?

Do you have an appropriate security policy in place to make sure that employees have access to only the data they require to perform their job function? This approach is "least-privilege" policy with role-based security.

What steps can you take to reduce the risk from common cyber threats?

18. The People!

Your greatest source of opportunity and risk lies with your staff. They do the work. They have the relationships. They have the special skill sets that are required. They also may be thieves! Kidding—sort of.

You can take some steps to protect your organization and its mission. Conduct background checks for each employee before he or she comes into your organization. You want to have a good understanding of potential employees' suitability for employment as they have access to your staff, your clients, your prospects, your plans, your "secret sauce," your data, and your physical assets.

- Put in place an employment agreement that emphasizes the confidentiality of the relationships and the information to which they have access. Make sure that your employees have clarity that anything they create while working for the organization is the property of the organization. If they have other "hobbies" that may have some conflict, make sure that they disclose those to you before the uncomfortable question arises of who owns what.

- Establish language in your client contracts that guards against your employees leaving to work for your clients or suppliers.

- Employment and contract law is an art form and varies by jurisdiction. Disputes in these areas are often resolved via costly legal battles. Get some help if you are unsure about what you can and should do in this regard.

Hands-On

Enumerate the employee and sub-contractor relationships in relation to your business.

Is the ownership of any work-product produced in those relationships clear and in writing?

Do you have an adequate agreement outlining the respective relationships between the organization and existing (and future) employees and sub-contractors?

Do you have reliable and appropriately-priced legal counsel to refer to for reviewing employment- and contract-related matters?

19. Staff Risks

Have clarity on which staff roles have access to specific data within your organization.

For sensitive data such as cash management, additional steps are recommended to reduce the likelihood of fraud or the unintentional damaging impact of a single resource making decisions which are not legal/appropriate/best for your business.

Here are some suggestions:

Job rotation: Rotate more than one person through a role.

Mandatory vacation: not all organizations can make this happen; however, this can be an excellent way to check on someone's work.

Double sign-off: make sure that financial transactions above a certain threshold require two signatures.

Dual control or split-function: make sure that two people need to be involved to conduct a transaction.

Conduct both periodic and surprise audits of work output.

Require detailed and summary reporting of transactions that is reviewed by supervisory personnel.

Employ a third-party bookkeeping service to review transactions.

Hands-On

What vulnerabilities does your organization have related to key operational staffing?

Are there policy changes you can introduce to reduce the risk of fraud in your organization?

Do you regularly train your staff on what proper process and behavior looks like?

Do you have a clearly-documented sanction policy for violations of proper actions?

20. Remote Access

It can be challenging to manage an employee when he or she is in the office. When employees are out of the office, it is even more challenging.

Beyond the basics of managing people remotely, consider the following:

1. How do you know that the person "logged in" to your office network is

    a. Really that person they claim to be (authentication)?

    b. Authorized to access the systems they are accessing?

2. Enable detailed audit logging.

3. Perform periodic and "spot" checks of authorized user and resource lists. Prune these lists aggressively.

4. Beware of common passwords for multiple systems. Once an employee or contractor leaves, it can be costly to have to change credentials. When feasible, it is best to provide unique credentials, tokens, or secure keys to each individual.

5. Ensure that remote workers do not use unsecured networks (WiFi or wired).

Hands-On

Do you have a clear policy on employee and subcontractor remote access?

Do you have an auto-expire policy on passwords to prevent age-old contractor and former employee credentials from accessing your network?

Do you have a policy regarding which devices can access your network remotely?

Do you have safeguards in place to permit remote workers to access only specific information pertinent to executing their job duties?

21. Remote and Mobile Worker Risks

Devices go missing.

Be sure to do the following:

- Put adequate passwords on all devices, including phones and tablets.

- Encrypt data on devices.

- Back up data on devices.

- If you are sending a device in for repair (e.g., Apple Store visit), be sure that your data is backed up and secure before going to the store.

- In a Bring-Your-Own-Device (BYOD) environment, be mindful of shoulder surfing and shared devices. Friends and family may have access to an employee's device, including all of the organization's sensitive data.

Hands-On

Does your organization have a clear policy on mobile device use?

Who in your organization is responsible for granting access to company information for mobile devices?

Do you have a secure means of disposing of mobile devices?

Are your laptops and tablets encrypted?

Do you have an inventory/asset tracking system to manage equipment issued to employees?

22. Data Loss Prevention

Data can leave our organizations in many unintended and unwanted ways. We can think of data in three states:

- **Data at rest:** Create an inventory of all sensitive data within the enterprise. Make sure your inventory includes software as a service (SaaS) and cloud services as well.

- **Data in motion:** Monitor the creation and movement of information across the enterprise.

- **Data in use:** Monitor (and limit) the usage of data on end-user equipment, with particular attention given to the use of this information on mobile devices.

For any data that is intended to be sent outside of your organization, make sure that there is a clearly-defined process, including who is permitted to perform the action and how the action is to take place, as well as when and why.

Any data manipulation and/or transfer outside of this process is to be reviewed as either a violation of the policy, or possibly a reason to expand the policy.

Hands-On

Do you know where all of the data resides in your organization?

Is there a documented process as to when, where, why, and through whom data is permitted to leave your organization?

Is there critical data in your organization that can be easily exfiltrated (in other words, removed from your network)? A common scenario is someone sitting down at a computer and emailing documents to his or her gmail.com account.

What steps can you take to reduce the threat of data loss in your organization?

Do you have clearly-defined consequences if your data-transfer policy is violated?

INDUSTRY

23. PCI-DSS

Payment Card Industry Data Security Standard (PCI-DSS)

- If you process payments from clients via credit or debit cards, you have an obligation to meet the requirements of PCI-DSS.

- PCI-DSS is an industry standard led by the likes of Visa.

- The requirements are non-trivial and for larger organizations there are full-time positions dedicated to nothing but PCI compliance.

- The penalties are serious.

- As a smaller organization start here:

    o Work with an experienced IT team (internal or outsourced) to manage your network.

    o Protect credit card data as if it were cash.

Put policies and procedures in place so the information does not go walking!

Hands-On

If you handle any credit card data, assume that you are required to comply with PCI-DSS until you determine that your organization is not required to adhere to the full PCI-DSS requirements. Hint: if you take credit cards, you are on the hook at some level.

Regardless of the size and volume of your credit card transactions, handle payment card information extremely carefully. Handle it with no less care than you expect someone to manage your own payment card information.

How can you better secure payment card data as it flows through your organization?

24. PCI-DSS Basics

PCI-DSS Requirements (https://www.pcisecuritystandards.org/pdfs/pci_ssc_quick_guide.pdf):

Build and maintain a secure network:
1. Install and maintain a firewall configuration to protect cardholder data.
2. Do not use vendor-supplied defaults for system passwords and other security parameters.

Protect cardholder data:
3. Protect stored cardholder data.
4. Encrypt transmission of cardholder data across open, public networks.

Maintain a vulnerability management program:
5. Use and regularly update anti-virus software on all systems commonly affected by malware.
6. Develop and maintain secure systems and applications.

Implement strong access control measures:
7. Restrict access to cardholder data on a need-to-know basis.
8. Assign a unique ID to each person with computer access (no shared credentials).
9. Restrict physical access to cardholder data.

Regularly monitor and test networks:
10. Track and monitor all access to network resources and cardholder data.
11. Regularly test security systems and processes.

Maintain an information security policy:
12. Maintain a policy that addresses information security.

Hands-On

Review your organization's information security controls from Chapter 7 and see how well they stack up to the PCI-DSS requirements.

Just because you have a firewall, do not assume that your network and your data are safe. On the assumption that a hacker got through your perimeter firewall, how easily could they access information on your network? Assume your outer defenses have been compromised. What do you need to do to secure your information? Think in layers.

What additional safeguards can you employ to protect not only your customer's payment data, but also your organization's reputation?

25. HIPAA/HITECH

Hospitals, physician practices, dental practices, and the like are Covered Entities. Covered Entities work with "Personal Health Information," or PHI.

"Business Associates" provide support services to Covered Entities and may come into contact with PHI.

Both Covered Entities and Business Associates have the same responsibility for the care and welfare of securing PHI.

Ask your business associates (and their suppliers) to execute a Business Associate Agreement (BAA). A BAA is a document which serves to notify everyone that the information being handled is sensitive and is to be treated appropriately.

Hands-On

Do you have up-to-date Business Associate Agreements in place with appropriate vendors and counter-parties?

If you are a business associate and make use of third-party vendors to deliver your services to a Covered Entity, do you have a BAA in place with your suppliers?

If the Health and Human Services Office of Civil Rights (HHS OCR) were to drop in for an audit of your organization, what would be your first step? Do you have a plan? Do you have a professional partner to assist you?

26. HIPAA/HITECH: The Big Rocks

Conduct an annual risk analysis.

Document what is working and what is out of compliance.

Create a work plan to address any gaps.

Measure your progress.

Establish Business Associate Agreements as appropriate with Covered Entities and "down-stream" Business Associates, as applicable.

Document your policies; train and test your employees regularly.

Have a formal sanction policy for any violations.

Encrypt your data on all devices, with a priority on mobile devices. Remember, your office may be vandalized and desktop computers stolen which contain PHI.

Have appropriate password policies in place.

Remember: don't assume you will be "lucky" and achieve compliance. Plan for it and manage it.

Hands-On

When was the last time you executed a risk analysis for your business?

Do you have a work plan to address identified gaps?

Have you documented the actions you have taken to remedy gaps in your compliance?

What is your next step toward compliance?

INFRASTRUCTURE & ORGANIZATION

27. Physical Conditions

The ideal temperature range for your computer equipment is between 68 and 75 °F. Relative humidity should be ± 50%. Generally speaking, if you are uncomfortable, your computer is uncomfortable also.

Monitor these values, ideally with some sort of historical charting and alarms.

Position your computer equipment away from places like bathrooms, and avoid placing them against an exterior wall as the sun load through the windows can easily overpower your HVAC system's ability to regulate the desired conditions.

Put your computer room in a location where you can readily see people coming and going.

Keep a computer room access log that records by whom, for what, when, why, and how long the room is being accessed.

Beware of using the cloud data center located in Miami, no matter how attractive the monthly rates.

Hands-On

Do you know the temperature and relative humidity of your computer room?

Do you know who has access to the computer room?

Do you store beverages or other liquids in your computer room?

What steps can you take to improve the physical security of your computer-related assets?

28. Wireless Network Security

Use modern equipment with up-to-date software.

Employ modern encryption protocols. Many older protocols have documented vulnerabilities.

Do not broadcast your network name (SSID).

Change your wireless password periodically. Use a strong password.

Have a separate wireless network for guests, and change its password frequently as well.

Manage internet bandwidth in such a manner that it does not impact your staff's day-to-day operations.

Periodically test your respective wireless networks so you know which devices are on each network.

Enable access logging.

Employ an enterprise wireless management platform, particularly if you have multiple locations where staff move between offices.

Be mindful of what resources are available via wireless networks. You may want to restrict access for wireless users.

Wireless devices that access your network may not belong to the company, and as such, pose additional attack vectors to your network.

Hands-On

Is your wireless network adequately secured?

How recently was your password changed?

Do you have a separate network for your guests?

Is your network security up to date, or is it using outdated technology?

Do your employees access your corporate network from public WiFi hotspots?

Do you change your wireless passwords when a device is reported to be lost or stolen?

Do you change your passwords when there is an employee termination or resignation?

29. Electronic Asset Lifecycle

Be intentional about asset management:

- Know what you own.

- Know who uses/controls each asset.

- Know the expected end-of-life date of each asset.

- Have a policy for asset decommissioning and disposal.

Hands-On

Do you have an up-to-date inventory of computer assets?

For each asset, do you know what information is stored on the equipment?

Do you know which user(s) make use of each asset?

Make sure you can answer these two questions with a satisfactory outcome for the long-term health and welfare of your organization and its mission:

1. If your equipment were to fail catastrophically, can you readily restore its function in a timely and non-business-impacting manner?

2. If your equipment were to be lost or stolen, and presumed to be in the hands of an arch-rival, can you both readily restore its function in a timely and non-business-impacting manner AND rest assured that there is no information readily accessible that will damage your organization's reputation or ability to pursue your mission?

Further, if equipment is lost or stolen, are you clear on any requirements you may have to meet by disclosing the incident to local, state, or federal authorities? For example, a laptop containing unencrypted Patient Health Information must be reported to state authorities.

30. Leased Equipment

Copiers, fax machines, and scanners pose an identity-theft threat.

Office machines in particular are a significant risk due to the fact that the contents of every page are written to the hard drive of the device. When the machine is returned to the leasing company, what happens to your data?

Understand what your flexibility is in terms of disposal and negotiate to get the features you need. A simple deletion of the data is not an adequate solution, even though the leasing company will likely assure you that this is the case.

The ideal scenario is that you retain the hard drive for destruction or get a certificate of destruction from the leasing company after you return the equipment.

Hands-On

Do you know who owns the office machines in your organization?

Do you have a contact name and working relationship with the owner of any leased equipment?

Do you have the disposal policy in writing from the owner of any leased equipment?

Have you attempted to buy out equipment in such a manner that you can ensure the proper disposal of storage media contained in leased equipment?

Have you trained your staff to understand the implications of the unauthorized use of leased equipment for the duplication and transmission of highly confidential information?

31. Computer Disposal

Don't throw your computers in the trash!

Destroy the hard drives:

- Encrypt the data with a strong algorithm and sufficiently random encryption key.

- Shred the hard drive; you can get a certificate of destruction from some vendors.

Make sure nothing is taped to the PC, monitor, or underside of the keyboard before you dispose of the device.

Beware of "hand-me-downs." It is okay to give your computers a noble second career. Just make sure your data does not go with them.

Hands-On

Do you have a policy on both sides of any computer exchanges (giving to others as well as receiving equipment)?

Do you have clarity on the origin and ownership of every piece of equipment in your organization? Be careful to not recycle leased equipment!

Have you given old equipment away to charities? Did you adequately destroy your data before disposing of the equipment?

Did you encrypt and/or destroy any hard drives before recycling old computer equipment?

Have you needed to return "bad" hardware to a retailer, distributor, or manufacturer? Did you properly dispose of any company data on the hard drive before shipping the equipment back?

32. Role-Based Security Management

The best practice for managing resource access is to employ role-based access control.

Establish groups by job function and/or business unit.

Create users on your network with unique user names and complex passwords. Use multi-factor authentication if feasible.

Place users into one or more group(s).

Assign privileges to the groups rather than to the individual users.

Periodically review the group membership lists to ensure that only active users are in the appropriate groups. Over time these lists can become bloated and include former employees who have long since left the organization.

Hands-On

Do you have a practice of reviewing which users have access to which data on a regular basis?

Do you have groups defined on your network where each group has access to specific assets and users are members in one or more group(s)?

Do you have a practice of granting "least privilege" to users?

What steps can you take to improve the posture of your users' access to data on your network?

33. Internet of Things & Industrial Control

Thermostats.

Copiers.

Refrigerators.

Cameras.

If it consumes electricity, assume that it may also connect to the internet.

That is both amazing and a challenge.

Not every product vendor takes security seriously. In fact, assume that the gadget you buy for your home or office is a vulnerability.

Do not casually enable "wireless" services.

If the device requires a password, do NOT use your email or work network password. You have no idea what the manufacturer is doing with this information. Assume that your credentials are backed up to a database at the manufacturer's offices. Or assume that a rogue hacker defeats the presumably weak defenses of your internet-connected device.

Hands-On

Look around your home and office. How many devices have internet connections? If you are having trouble determining this, look at your internet router—most devices will automatically get an IP address on your network that is distributed by your router or server.

For each device, make sure you know exactly which features are enabled. If possible, monitor inbound and outbound traffic. A seemingly "dumb" internet-enabled camera may be a perfect means for a remote hacker to extract critical company information.

For each network-controlled device, ask yourself, "What would happen if that device turned on (or off) at an undesirable time?"

Is there a "manual override" feature permitting you to use the device in the event that network connectivity were lost?

What steps can you take to better secure your network with respect to "internet-connected" devices?

34. Multi-Factor Authentication

A password is better than no password.

A complex password is better than a simple password.

Biometrics (iris, retina, fingerprint, etc.) can be better than passwords, but they can be very expensive to implement well and may be too error-prone in certain circumstances.

The best approach is "multi-factor authentication (MFA)," where you need to provide two or more of the following:

- Something you know (password)

- Something you have (key fob/token of some variety)

- Something you are (biometric)

Enforce lock-out policies if possible. For example, do not let an attacker try 10,000 passwords in a brute-force attack.

Enable intelligent system access logging that will not only record login attempts but will also "auto-ban" attackers.

Beware of making users change their passwords too frequently. This leads to trivialization of passwords that are easier to crack.

Hands-On

Do you have a complex password policy enabled on your network?

Do you have a password expiration policy?

Do you employ a multi-factor authentication approach?

What steps can you take to improve authentication to your computer-based assets?

35. Configuration and Change Management

Keep a detailed (and secured) inventory of all electronic and information-related assets, including the following:

- Hardware warranty dates

- SaaS credentials

- Software licenses and renewal dates

- Downloadable software (software keys are usually emailed and then lost in the noise of someone's inbox)

- A list of employee/staff skills

Changes or customizations made to software packages

Hands-On

Do you have clarity on where all of your passwords, serial numbers, account numbers, and other important information reside? Is this information secure?

Who in your organization is responsible for gathering and maintaining this information?

Is this information backed up?

Is this information tracked with versioning and/or effective dates?

What information is missing from your list?

Review each job function in your organization and ask yourself which resources employees make use of in order to perform their job duties.

For a given resource (e.g., Salesforce.com or Indeed.com), do you have only a single account with full access, or do you have properly-delegated access for each user?

Do you have a well-defined process to follow when you add a new service or retire an existing service from use by your organization?

What do you do when an employee leaves the company? Do you need to scramble and guess at which passwords to change, or do you have a well-defined and audited process?

SOFTWARE CONCERNS

36. Custom Software Development

If your organization generates custom software, you will want to enforce the use of a software development methodology; i.e., a standard approach to how your organization develops software and manages changes to it over time.

Utilize source code management tools (git, svn, etc.)

Maintain production and testing environments.

Automate the deployment process.

Fully document the dependencies of your software.

Beware of a single point of vulnerability; e.g., only one programmer who knows how everything works.

Make it a practice to keep up to date on industry trends.

Subscribe to industry newsletters, particularly those focused on security practices and vulnerabilities.

Hands-On

If your primary programmer suddenly resigned what are the implications for your team?

Do you own all of the source code for your offering? If not, do you have an agreed-upon process to obtain access to it as business needs may require in the future?

Do you have a full understanding of all third-party dependencies in your product or service?

Do you have appropriate licenses for the manner in which third-party software is used in your products? For example, software licenses are commonly managed on either a developer basis, a domain name basis, or on an OEM basis.

Do you have metrics on your software development process?

Is your team regularly trained on best practices in the Software Development Life Cycle (SDLC)?

37. Common Security Issues in Software

SQL Injection attacks

Operating System Injection attacks

Cross-site scripting attacks

Unrestricted file uploads

Permitting execution of code in file upload directories

Lack of input checking

Path Transversal

Lack of code download signatures and checksums

Lack of granular controls

Hard-coded credentials

Permissions granted to application users excessively

Lack of logging

Simplistic use of hashing and encryption algorithms

Hands-On

Does your software development team conduct peer code reviews?

Do you perform regular testing of your code before deployment?

Do you review each of the common security issues on a regular basis?

Is there any "low-hanging fruit" you can target for quickly improving the security posture of your software assets?

38. Software Operational Issues

Beware of multiple versions of the same application in use. If there is a problem, where did it come from, and how do you remedy it?

Beware that your logging is neither too little or too much.

- Too little does not provide enough value when trying to track down a problem.

- Too much logging may either:

    o Store sensitive information in an area where it can be viewed by unauthorized personnel.

    o Eat up your storage quickly and place your operational systems at further risk.

All activity should take place through written and tested software via well-formed transactions. Beware of manual changes made directly in the database! This is known as the Clark Wilson integrity model, which states that you should have "well-formed transactions." Editing data manually in a file or database is likely not a well-formed transaction.

Hands-On

Are there any transactions where users can see more data than the minimum they require to perform their job duties?

Do you regularly review log files for anomalies? Are there opportunities to automate these review steps?

Do you have clearly-documented steps for installing each version of software in use in your enterprise?

If an unauthorized user were to gain access to your log files, would he or she find information that would compromise your mission?

What steps can you take to improve the operational readiness of your organization as it relates to the management of the software in use?

39. Capability Maturity Model for Software

Over time your software development process should mature. See this image of the Capability Maturity Model for Software:

Level		Capability	Result
5	Optimizing	**Continuous Process Improvement** Organizational Innovation & Deployment Causal Analysis & Resolution	**Productivity & Quality**
4	Quantitatively Managed	**Quantitative Management** Quantitative Process Management Software Quality Management	
3	Defined	**Process Standardization** Requirements Development Technical Solution Product Integration Verification Validation Organizational Process Focus Organizational Process Definition Organizational Training Integrated Product Management Risk Management Integrated Teaming Integrated Supplier Management Decision Analysis & Resolution Organizational Environment for Integration	
2	Managed	**Basic Project Management** Requirements Management Project Planning Project Monitoring & Control Supplier Agreement Management Measurement & Analysis Product & Process Quality Assurance Configuration Management	
1	Initial	**Heroic Efforts** Design Develop Integrate Test	**Risk & Waste**

(http://1stmuse.com/sw/capability_maturity_model/) Over time, your team's experience should move from the lower portions described here as "heroic efforts" and move toward a measurable, improving process of adding features and capabilities to the benefit of your organization.

Hands-On

Where is your organization in terms of its maturity for software development?

What benefits can you envision to your mission if your organization were operating at the highest level of this maturity model?

What steps are you taking to improve this key aspect of your business?

WRAPPING UP

40. Recommended Practices

Use multi-factor authentication whenever possible.

Create strong passwords and change them periodically (but not too often).

Never use the same password on more than a single system.

Use anti-virus and anti-malware tools. Keep them up to date.

Install only software you need and only from trusted sources.

Avoid/limit social media disclosure of information, particularly if you are a HIPAA Covered Entity.

Delete email from anyone you do not know who is asking anything suspicious—take a conservative and cautious posture.

Be especially vigilant around email attachments, particularly from people you do know, as the email may not be actually from them!

Do not be afraid to pick up the phone and speak with a counter-party if you suspect something about an email.

Put passwords on all of your devices, including phones and tablets.

Make sure lock-screens activate quickly when you are away from your computer.

Hands-On

Have you clearly communicated to your staff the "best practices" of safe online activity?

Do you test your staff on proper online behavior?

What steps will you take to help safeguard your organization through user training?

41. Get Some Help and Try Not to Be So Gullible!

Enable alerts from your bank and credit card company. American Express and other credit card companies will send you an email anytime there is a "card not present" transaction.

Review your bank statements. Require everyone on your team to document their online purchases, particularly from large retailers where the transaction record may be ambiguous, making it difficult to reconcile weeks later by a book-keeper.

Do not panic if/when you see an email from the bank, the IRS, the collection agency, or even your friend who claims to be stuck in London without his or her wallet. Do not click through the email in haste to learn more or to help. If you think there may be a legitimate issue, be sure to call the appropriate office using a known good number.

Do not hit "redial" on the 800 number claiming to be the American Express fraud department. Using the phone number on the back of your credit card is the best policy as an internet search result may be faked as well. If you are the subject of an Advanced Persistent Threat (APT), you may not be able to trust a Google search result from your office.

If the government really wants to get your attention, it will not be via email.

Hands-On

Do you have clarity on the safeguards and services available from your banks and credit card providers?

Which employees in your organization have access to crucial online financial information such as bank accounts, credit cards, and taxation authority websites?

What steps will you take to reduce embarrassing mistakes from impacting your organization?

Have you practiced an "incident response" to know how your team should react in the event of a damaging incident?

42. Be Open Anyway

There is no foolproof way of stopping all cyber crime.

Even if you were to "air-gap" your machine, i.e., unplug it from any network, Ethan Hunt from the Impossible Mission Force may drop through the ceiling one day and steal the information. More likely someone in your organization, possibly you, may use a thumb-drive to side-step the annoyance of a "disconnected" device.

If you have information about which you would be aghast if someone else read it, think twice before creating that information. Assume that all of your information will be laid bare for the world to see at some point, so be sure to keep that in mind when you create it in the first place.

Hands-On

Imagine your mom, your employees, and your primary competitor have access to your email, voicemail, and browsing history. What do you feel? Would you do anything differently?

What will you change about your communication practices to better improve your posture with respect to cyber crime?

About the Author

Frank Ableson is a husband, father, and entrepreneur. On a good day he's getting all of those done. Every other day, he's thankful for grace, a sense of humor, and when necessary, forgiveness.

For more information or help in your next IT decision, visit http://www.navitend.com.

Made in the USA
Middletown, DE
12 November 2023

42457723R00073